now you know

HOW iT WORKS

for David
engineer extraordinaire

AUTHOR'S NOTE

For the purposes of creating this book, I chose simple and accessible explanations over depth and complexity so that it would be engaging and informative to the youngest of readers. My hope is that by revealing some of the engineering and physics of everyday objects, I will spark children's curiosity and inspire them to keep asking, "How does that work?"

Special thanks to Dr. Peter Wong, PhD, Director of Food Initiative and Special Assistant to the president at the Museum of Science in Boston, MA, for his guidance and expert verification of the information included in this book.

This edition first printing, January 2019

Book design by Valorie Fisher and Kirk Benshoff

12 11 10 9 8 7 6 5 4 3 2
19 20 21 22 23 24

Printed in the U.S.A.   40

now you know

HOW IT WORKS

valorie fisher

SCHOLASTIC INC.

What's inside this book

How to read this book

 A combination of **A** and **B** equals **C**.

 A comes from or can be found in **B**.

 Dotted line with arrows shows the flow or path of airflow, energy, liquid, or electricity in that direction.

 Solid line with an arrow shows direction of an object.

 Short arrow shows an action or an action's direction.

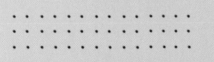 Pattern of dots shows air pressure.

 At the bottom of some pages, you will find a circle with an image inside. This image means that a process or concept mentioned on this page has also been mentioned on the page with that image in the circle. Go to that circle's page to check it out!

Rubber Ball

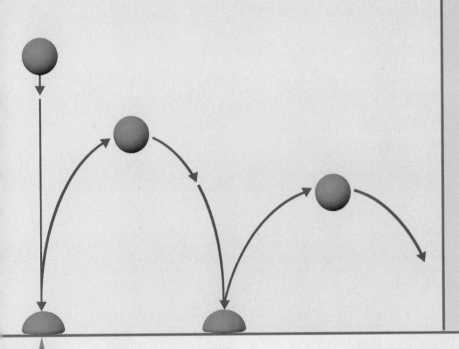

rubber ball

=

latex

made from
sap of the
rubber tree

Rubber is an **elastic** material that can store energy. This means it can change shape and quickly return to its original shape.

When a rubber ball drops to the ground, it gains speed and motion **energy**. With each bounce, the ball loses a little energy, but some stays inside the squished ball. The energy inside the ball causes it to spring back up and return to its original shape.

Bicycle

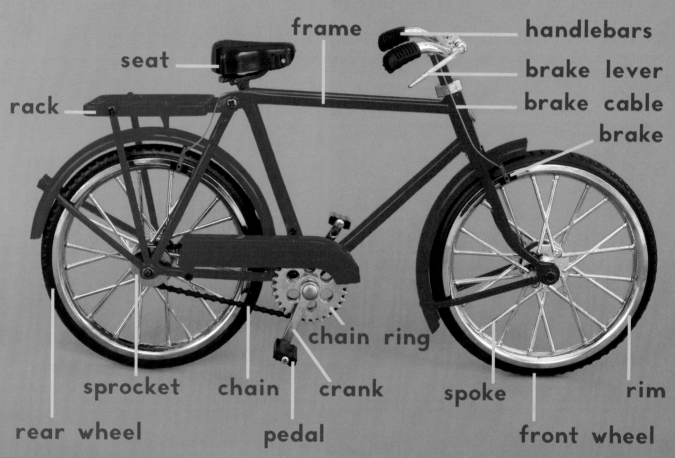

seat

rack

frame

handlebars

brake lever

brake cable

brake

chain ring

sprocket   chain   crank   spoke   rim

rear wheel   pedal   front wheel

brakes

Squeezing the brake lever pulls the brake cable, which causes the brake pads to clamp together on the rim. When the brake pads clamp together on the rim, the bicycle slows down.

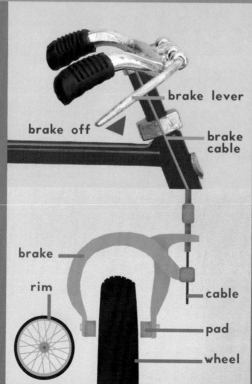

brake lever

brake off

brake cable

brake

rim

cable

pad

wheel

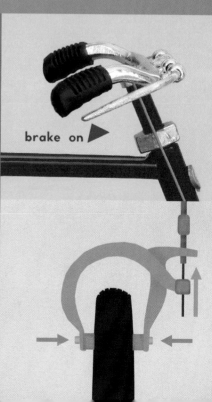

brake on

Bicycle

rear wheel

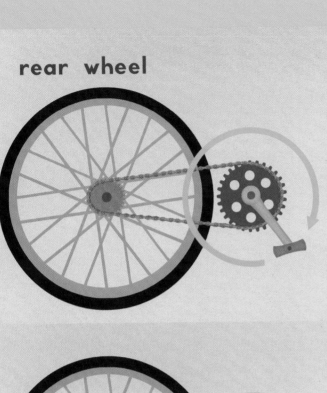

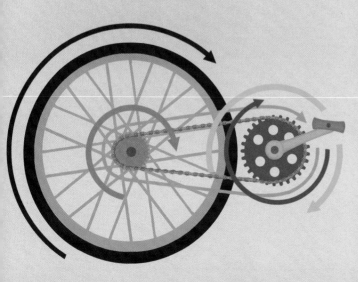

front wheel

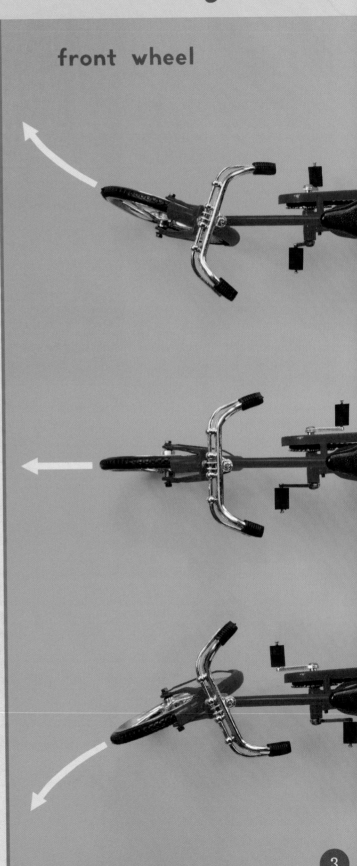

3

Light passes through an object that is **transparent**, or see-through.

Light does not pass through an object that is **opaque**, or not see-through. The blocked light creates a shadow.

EAST

midday

WEST

morning

afternoon

Your shadow changes shape and position throughout the day as the sun moves across the sky from east to west.

sunrise

sunset

Light Bulb

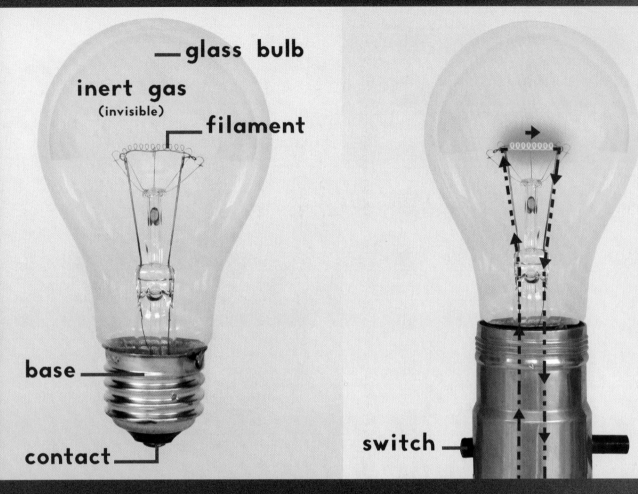

glass bulb

inert gas
(invisible)

filament

base

contact

switch

The **filament** is a thin metal wire. When a light is switched on, **electricity** flows to the light bulb up to the filament, making the filament very hot. The filament glows, creating light. The bulb is filled with an inert gas, which allows the filament to glow without burning up.

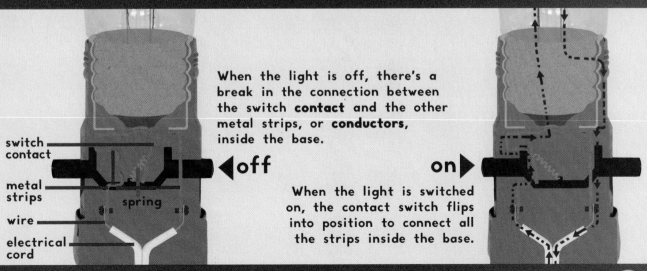

switch contact

metal strips

spring

wire

electrical cord

◀off

on▶

When the light is off, there's a break in the connection between the switch **contact** and the other metal strips, or **conductors**, inside the base.

When the light is switched on, the contact switch flips into position to connect all the strips inside the base.

When the light is on, electricity flows from the outlet ➝ electrical cord ➝ metal strips ➝ bulb ➝ filament.

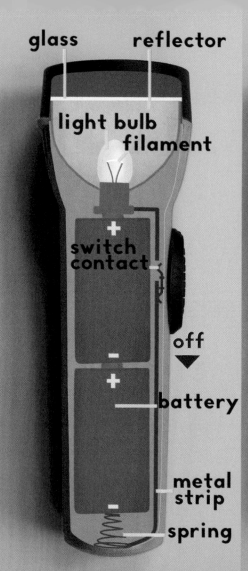

glass   reflector

light bulb
filament

switch
contact

+

–

+

off

battery

–

metal
strip

spring

switch

case

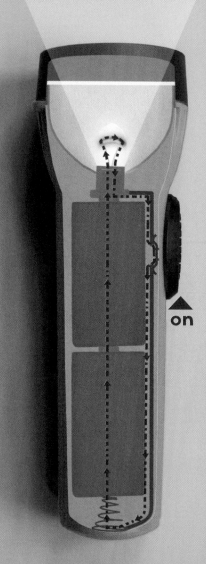

on

When the flashlight switch is on, contact is made. Electricity flows from metal strip
---------> spring --------> batteries --------> bulb --------> filament.

reflector

light bulb

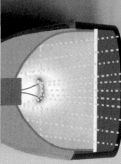

light

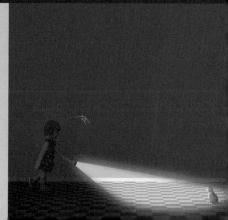

The curved and shiny surface of the **reflector**
helps direct and focus the light, creating a
more intense widening beam of light.

6

straw —

You may not always feel it, but air pushes on everything it comes in contact with. This is called air **pressure**.

1

air pressure ▬

At first, the air pressure in the glass and in the straw are equal.

2

When you sip, the air pressure in the straw decreases.

3

The air pressure in the glass is greater than the air pressure in the straw.

4

The difference in pressure causes the juice to be pushed up into the straw.

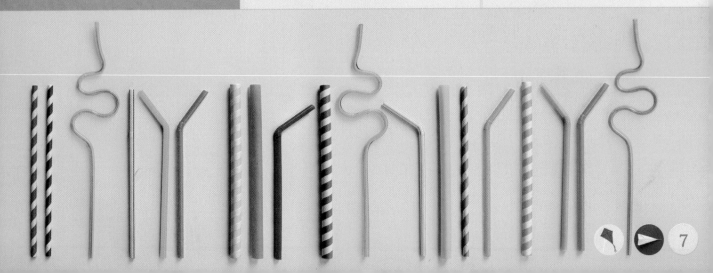

Paper Airplane

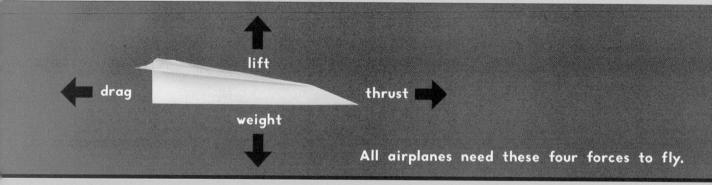

lift

drag

thrust

weight

All airplanes need these four forces to fly.

The force of throwing the airplane moves it forward, creating thrust.

thrust

Air moving across the wings creates more air pressure underneath the airplane than above it, creating lift.

lift

air pressure

Air creates **resistance**, slowing the airplane down, creating drag.

drag

The weight of the airplane affects how quickly it comes down.

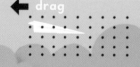

weight

Paper Airplane

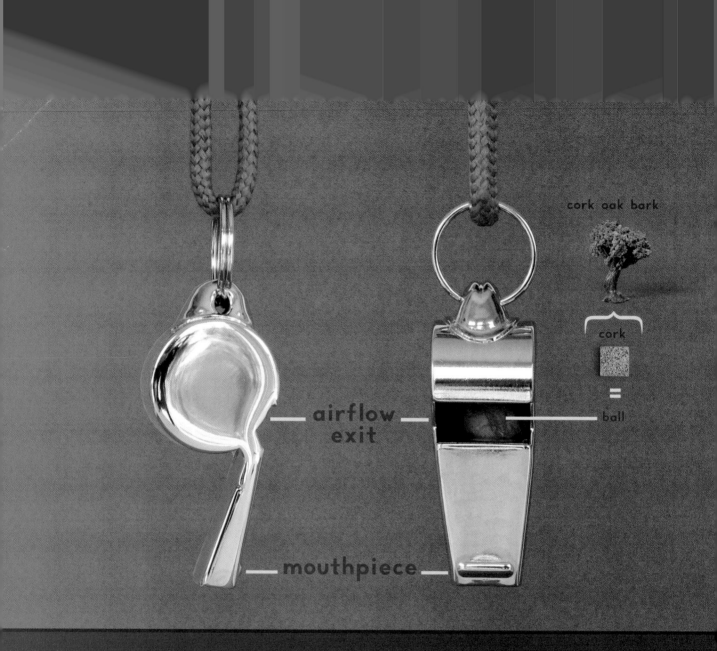

cork oak bark

cork

=

ball

airflow exit

mouthpiece

Air flowing through the whistle splits as it strikes the edge of the opening. This split causes the air to swirl and **vibrate** in the chamber, creating a high-pitched sound as it exits.

The air swirls and vibrates in the chamber, causing the ball to spin and bounce. The ball bouncing and bumping into the airflow creates the trill sound.

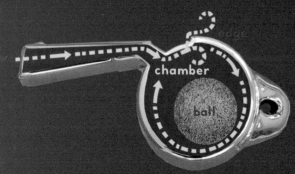

airflow

edge

chamber

ball

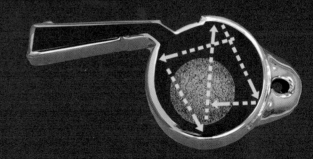

high-pitched sound + trill sound = unique whistle sound

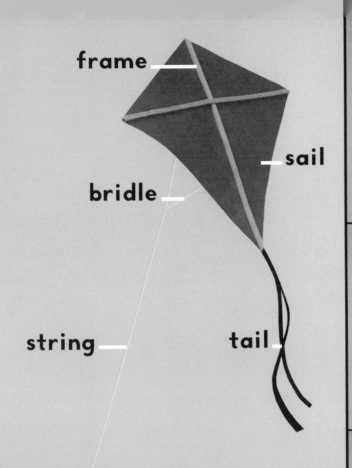

frame

sail

bridle

string

tail

spool

lift

Air flowing above and below the kite creates more pressure below and helps get it into the air. This is lift.

weight

The weight of the kite pulls it back to the ground. Lightweight materials help a kite fly. This is weight.

- - wind - - - - - →
wind - - - - - →
- - wind - - →

thrust

Pulling the string tight as the wind blows across the kite helps the kite stay in the air. This is thrust.

drag

Air moving across the surfaces creates more pressure in front of the kite, which creates resistance. This slows down the kite. This is drag.

Toilet

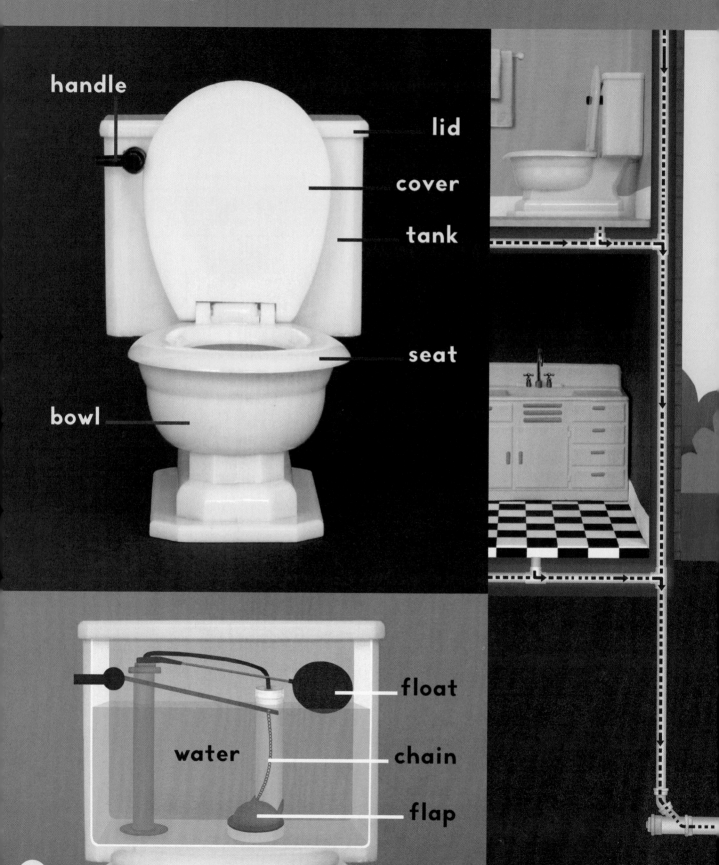

handle

lid

cover

tank

seat

bowl

float

water

chain

flap

1

When you press the handle down, the flap opens and water quickly flows into the bowl.

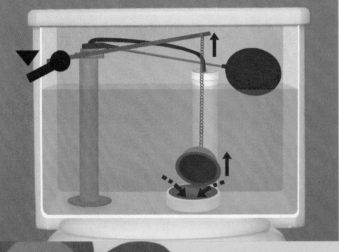

2

Water fills the bowl, pushing up the trapway. The shape and position of the bend in the trapway create a sucking effect. Water rushes over the bend and sucks the rest of the water out of the bowl.

bend
trapway
water pipe
drain

3

As the water drains, the flap closes. The float lowers, triggering the flow of water from the water pipe to refill the tank.

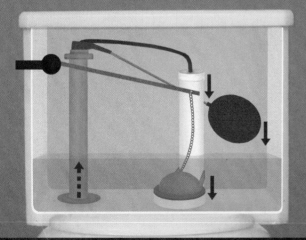

4

Water fills the tank until the float rises, shutting off the flow of water to the tank.

Garbage

compost

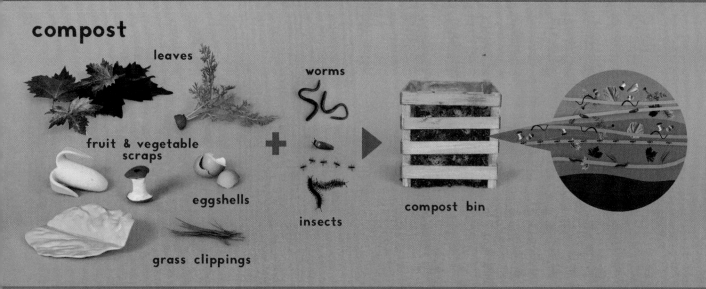

leaves

worms

fruit & vegetable scraps

eggshells

insects

compost bin

grass clippings

recycling

cardboard

plastic

Crunchy Corn

SPAGHETTI

THIS SIDE UP

LOCALLY GROWN

metal

SUPER CLEAN Dish Soap

WE RECYCLE

Neighborhood RECYCLE

paper

glass

FARM FRESH MILK

recycle bin

Trucks collect the recycling and bring it to a landfill.

trash

food scraps

broken dishes

light bulb

bandages

Styrofoam

plastic utensils

TRASH DISPOSAL

trash bin

Trucks collect the trash and bring it to a landfill.

14

packaging

hanger

Worms and insects help by eating, pooping, and tunneling their way through the compost pile. This helps the plants and food **decompose**. Many months later, the compost is ready to use, helping plants grow strong and healthy.

compost

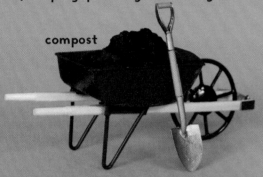

The compost is rich in nutrients, and is a natural fertilizer for the garden.

At the recycling center, the recycling is sorted and sent to factories to be processed.

Glass, metals, and plastics are crushed, chopped, and melted. Papers and cardboards are shredded and washed. After they are processed, they are made into new products.

parts of

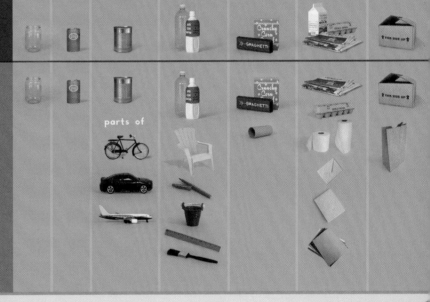

At the landfill, the trash is dumped and moved into huge piles. There is a layer of plastic under the trash that protects the soil below. When the landfill is full, the piles are covered with another protective layer of plastic and then covered with soil.

Blender

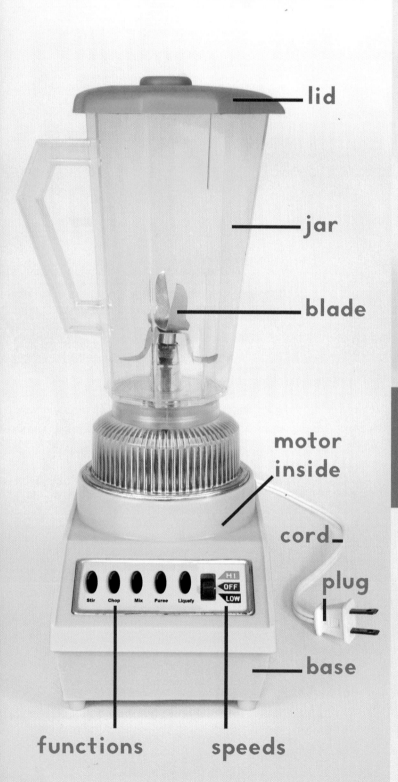

lid

jar

blade

motor
inside

cord

plug

base

| Stir | Chop | Mix | Puree | Liquefy | HI OFF LOW |

functions   speeds

Spinning very fast, the blade slices and mixes, creating an upward spiral. As the mixture reaches the top it moves inward, spiraling down and then back up in a continuous loop, like a tornado.

When a blender is switched on, electricity powers the motor, spinning the blade.

Pencil

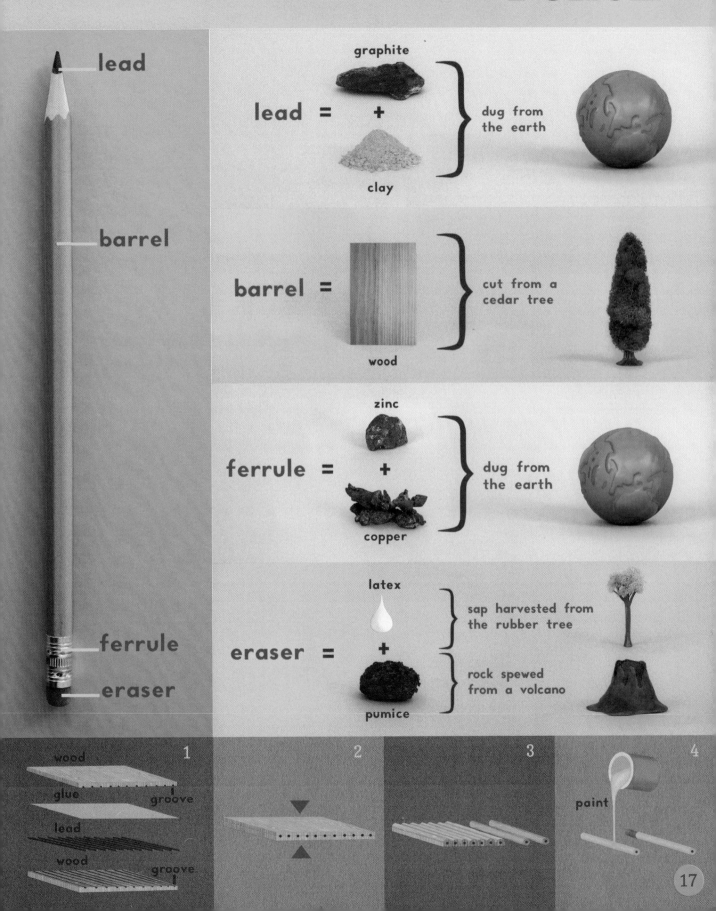

lead

barrel

ferrule

eraser

lead = graphite + clay } dug from the earth

barrel = wood } cut from a cedar tree

ferrule = zinc + copper } dug from the earth

eraser = latex } sap harvested from the rubber tree
+ pumice } rock spewed from a volcano

1 wood glue groove lead wood groove

2

3

4 paint

17

Pencil Sharpener

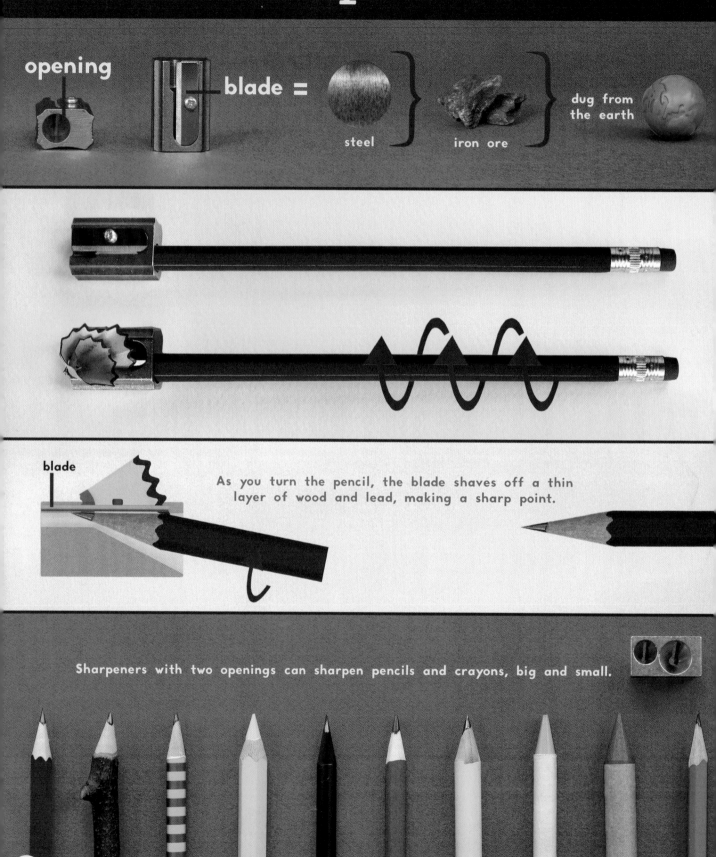

opening

blade = steel } iron ore } dug from the earth

blade

As you turn the pencil, the blade shaves off a thin layer of wood and lead, making a sharp point.

Sharpeners with two openings can sharpen pencils and crayons, big and small.

Toaster

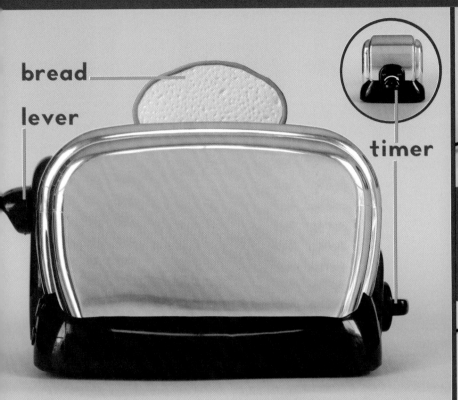

bread

lever

timer

wire

tray   catch

When the toast is placed in the slot, it sits on top of a tray. Pressing down the lever lowers the spring, which lowers the tray. The catch holds it in place.

The lever presses the contacts together and starts the flow of electricity through the wires that line the toast slots. The wires become hot and toast the bread.

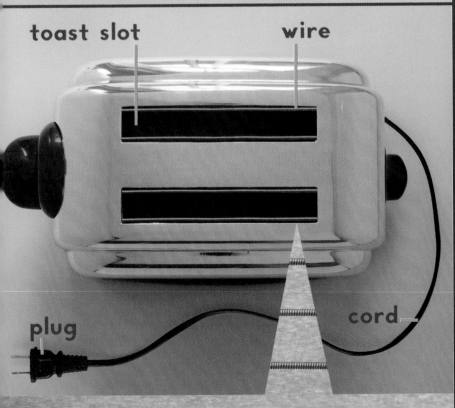

toast slot   wire

plug   cord

The toast slots are lined with rows of thin nichrome wires, which become hot with the flow of electricity.

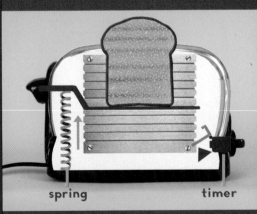

spring   timer

When the toast is done, a timer releases the catch. The spring pops up, raising the tray and the toast.

Thermometer

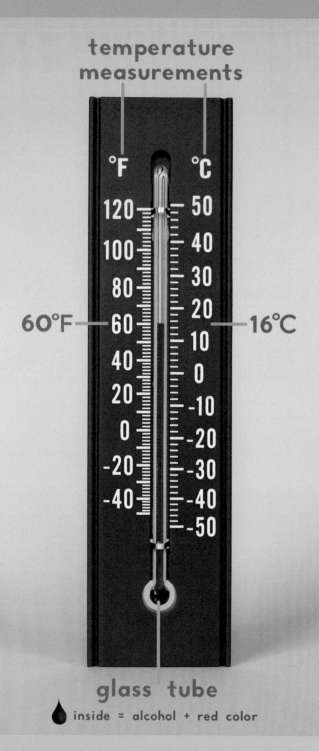

temperature
measurements

°F   °C

60°F—60 20—16°C

glass tube

● inside = alcohol + red color

Alcohol reacts to temperature change.
It **expands**, or gets bigger, in the heat,
and **contracts**, or gets smaller, in the
cold. Red coloring added to the alcohol
makes it easier to see.

100°F—100 40—38°C

When it's hot out, the alcohol
expands, moving up the glass tube.

20°F—20   -7°C

When it's cold out, the alcohol
contracts, moving down the glass tube.

°F Fahrenheit and °C Celsius are different scales used to measure temperature.

Thermometer

A cricket can tell you the temperature.
As temperatures rise, a cricket becomes
increasingly active, and chirps more
frequently. By counting a cricket's chirps,
you can calculate the temperature.

Count the number
of chirps a cricket
makes in 14 seconds.

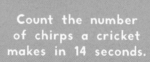 14 seconds

chirps + 40°F = temperature in °F

chirps/14 seconds	+ 40°F =	temperature °F
15		55
20		60
25		65
30		70
35		75
40		80
45		85
50		90

Soap

Some soaps have added color and fragrance

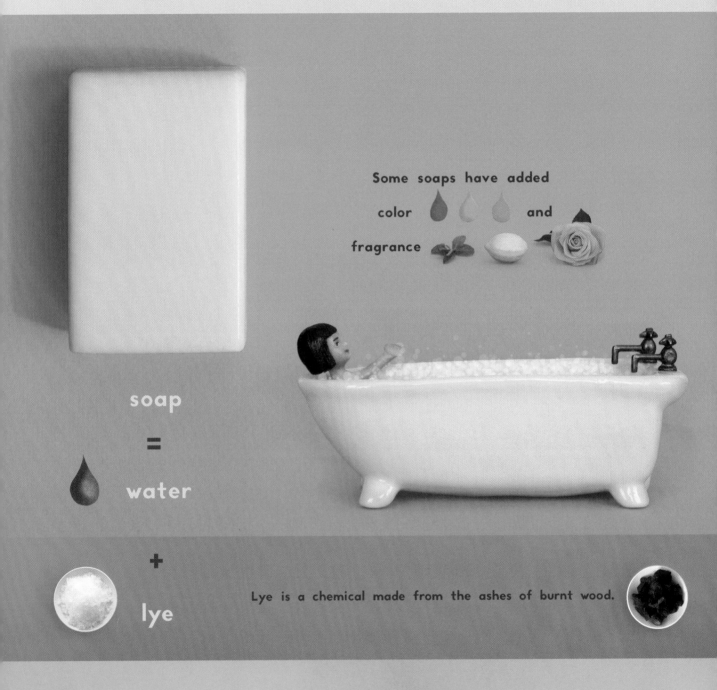

soap

=

water

+

lye

Lye is a chemical made from the ashes of burnt wood.

+

fatty oil

Fatty oils are made from the fruit, seeds, and nuts of plants.

olive   coconut   avocado   peanut   sunflower

Crayon

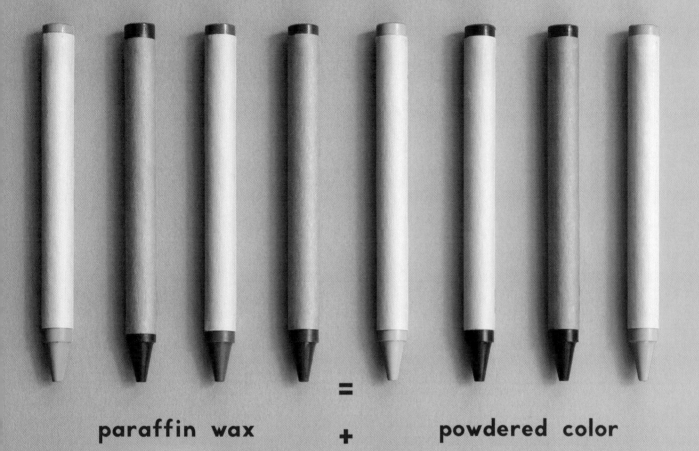

paraffin wax + **powdered color**

Paraffin wax is made from petroleum oil.

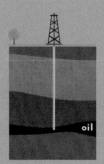

oil

Petroleum oil was created from decomposed plants and animals

Petroleum oil is drilled from deep inside the earth.

that lived millions of years ago, even before dinosaurs.

Powdered colors are often made from natural sources.

slate   iron ore   minerals

23

Boat

An object in water will either float or sink.

water

sink

float

The weight of an object in water pushes the water out of the way.

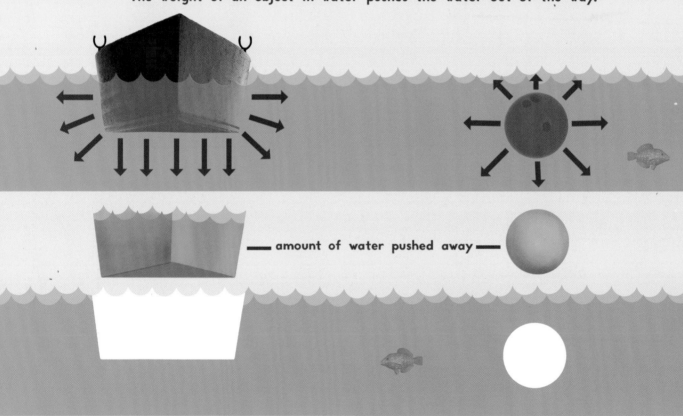

amount of water pushed away

The boat floats because it weighs the same as the weight of the water it pushed away.

The bowling ball sinks because it weighs more than the weight of the water it pushed away.

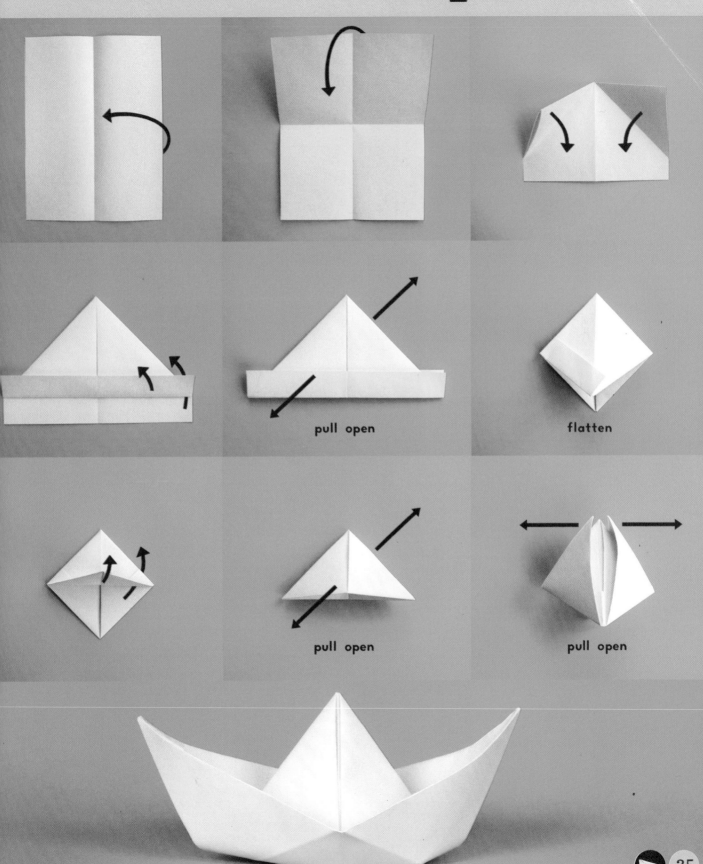

pull open

flatten

pull open

pull open

Screw

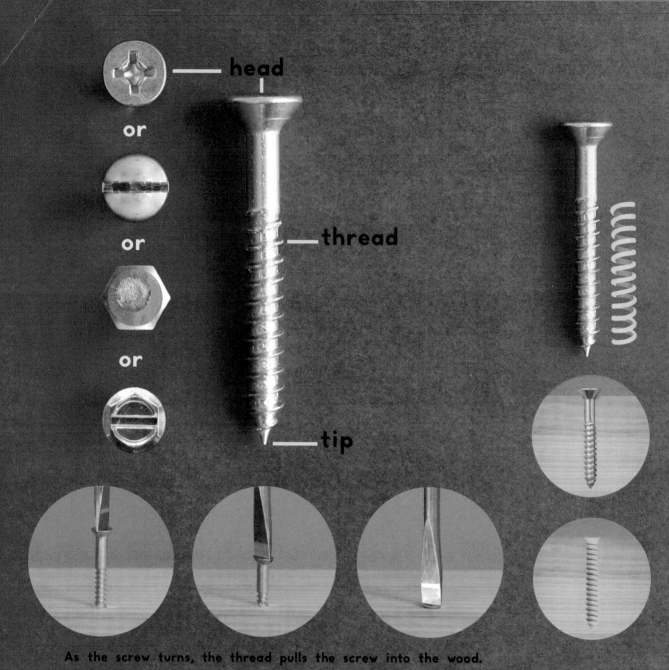

head

thread

tip

or

or

or

As the screw turns, the thread pulls the screw into the wood.

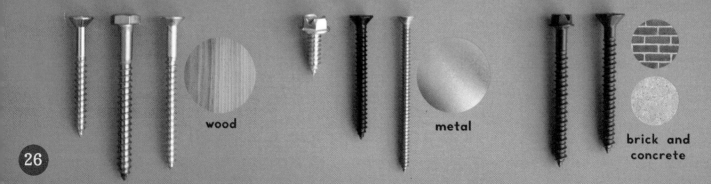

wood

metal

brick and concrete

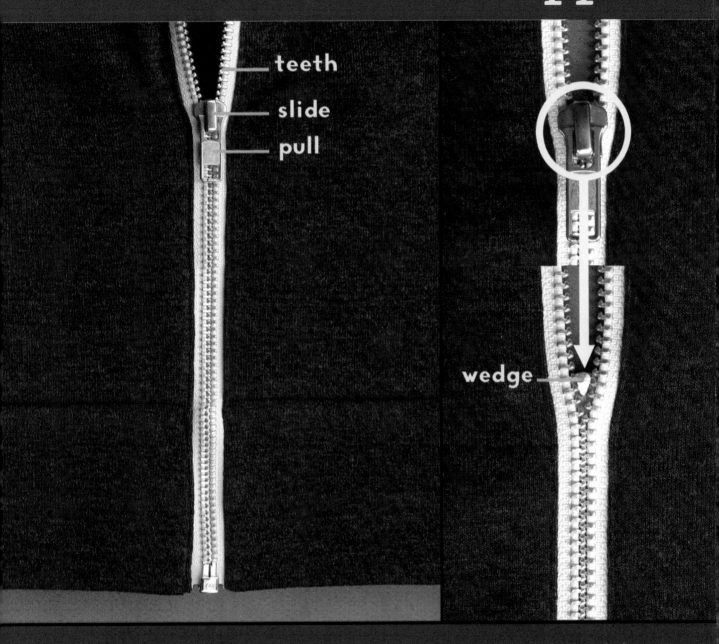

teeth

slide

pull

wedge

As the slide is pulled up, the wedge pulls the hook-shaped teeth together, and they **interlock**, closing the zipper. As the slide is pulled down, the wedge forces the teeth apart, opening the zipper.

2

3

Words to Know

conductor

A conductor is a material or substance that allows electricity to flow through it. Metals are often good conductors.

copper wire

copper

contact

Contact is the state of touching someone or something. In this book, the contact is the point where the conductors touch to allow the flow of electricity.

contact

contact

contract

To contract is to get smaller. When you let the air out of a balloon it contracts.

1   2

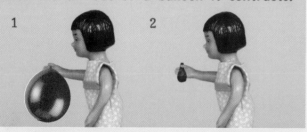

decompose

To decompose is to break down or rot. The apple was left out for too long and started to decompose.

1   2

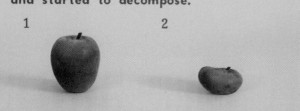

elastic

If a material is elastic, it is able to be stretched or squished and then return to its original shape. A rubber band is elastic.

1   2   3

electricity

Electricity is a form of energy that is used to make light, heat, and power for machines.

energy

Energy is the ability of something to do work. There are many different kinds of energy. When a ball bounces, it is using energy.

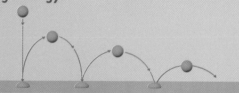

expand

To expand is to get bigger. When you blow air into a balloon it expands.

1   2

filament

A filament is a very thin wire that electricity flows through. It can get very hot without melting.

filament

reflector

A reflector is a shiny, often textured surface for reflecting and directing light. Car headlights have reflectors.

interlock

To interlock is to fit together. When you put your hands together, your fingers interlock.

resistance

Resistance is the force that works in opposition to, or against, the way an object is moving. Cycling is easy on the road, but not on the sand. The sand creates resistance.

1   2

opaque

An opaque object is not see-through and light cannot pass through it. A bowling ball is opaque.

transparent

A transparent object is see-through, or clear, and light can pass through it. A fish bowl is transparent.

pressure

Pressure is the force of one thing pressing on another. Putting pressure on the toothpaste tube squeezes the toothpaste out.

vibrate

To vibrate is to move back and forth very quickly. When you pluck a guitar string, it vibrates.